UNTRAMMELED VISION

An Introduction into Covert Surveillance Operations

By: Vincent E. Green

Retired Deputy Commissioner New York City Department of Investigation and Director of Investigator Training

G-SQUARE PUBLISHING
Department of Integrity and
Anti-Corruption

Contents

Preface

The information provided in this publication has been compiled from the combined experience of more than 40 years of the author in conducting physical and electronic surveillance operations. That being said, it should be understood that this publication merely touches on the basics of surveillance.

Please keep in mind that as technology changes and the connections between corrupt acts expand locally, nationally, and globally, the way in which investigators conduct surveillances must adjust to fit the situation. Many corruption schemes have international connections. Planning such operations as undercover operations, interviews, interrogations and surveillance must be approached with a global mindset.

Surveillance is not just about following; it is about culture, economics, ideologies, values, ethics, and piecing the puzzle together. How to conduct surveillance does not come in a box, on a flash drive, or in a manual. Those things are just a foundation upon which to build. The way that an investigator learns how to conduct surveillance is by doing surveillance.

The skill required in conducting surveillance is very much akin to that required for the game of chess. As with chess, not everyone is good at it.

Another distinguishing fact is that while chess might be an interesting game, surveillance is by no stretch of the imagination a game. Surveillance is an art; it requires a multidimensional approach to thinking to be successful.

Let's start by saying; never begin from the premise that surveillance begins when the person of interest comes out of their home, place of business, or wherever it has been decided that the actual observation of the target will begin. If that is the approach applied, then it will be checkmate in a few poorly executed moves.

An accomplished investigator understands that the key to successful surveillance is not just execution but also preparation. Understand that the driving skills an investigator may possess and the investigator's ability at coming up with disguises, while significant, mean manifestly nothing if the proper research has not been done.

CHAPTER 1
Definitions
"Each man must be his own purveyor of truth."
Vinny Green

It has been said that no facet of investigative work is more open to improvement through practice than the techniques used in conducting surveillance. Surveillance is not, and should not be, regarded as a haphazard "hit or miss" operation. Prior preparation and planning are essential because once the operation has commenced, opportunities to reorganize it are extremely challenging. Given the existence of this difficulty, it is of paramount importance to understand why surveillance is being done and how it is to be executed.

Execution of the operation must begin by understanding the language of surveillance and the meaning of terms and phrases employed in the surveillance process. Like all aspects of investigations, communication is key. It is a good idea to understand some of the basic terminologies used in conducting surveillance:

Burned: This is a term used when the person of interest has identified a surveillance team member. Do not assume that the target will always let it be known that they have been alerted to the surveillance.

However, there are times that the target will let it be known in visible ways and possibly even in a physical and hostile way. Be sensitive to this possibility.

Choke Points: To pick up a surveillance subject from the place of greatest congestion, if taking the subject from home or some other location, is not feasible.

In terms of surveillance operations, the choke point, also known as a bottleneck, is an area in either the subject's neighborhood, work location, or frequented location where the subject is likely to have to pass through because of the design of the streets, roads, construction, or exits out of the area.

It is that point which the subject has to traverse in order to get to where they might be going, like a highway, subway entrance, bridge, or tunnel.

It is, in essence, the point that you know the subject will have to use in the event that you have lost them, or circumstances will not allow you to set up in the neighborhood.

Cleaning: This is the process whereby the subject of surveillance takes action to lose the surveillance believed to be in play or to make sure that people or vehicles are not engaging in surveillance.

Committed: This is when the subject of the surveillance is committed to a move being made, such as entering a highway or making a turn.

Contact: Contacts are individuals whom the target meets during the course of the surveillance. It is necessary to make detailed notes of all observed contacts. It is likely that one or more of these individuals will appear in subsequent surveillance, or possibly even in counter surveillance. Contacts may lead an investigative team to new information or confirm suspicions about old information.

Counter surveillance: This is surveillance used by the target to detect surveillance focused on them.

Counter surveillance *Maneuvers:* This implies that the subject or conspirator is engaging in tactics designed to detect, if not defeat, tactics being used by the surveillance team.

Critical Situation: A situation that comes up during surveillance that presents an immediate possibility of detection or danger.

Looking for Heat: The subject of the surveillance appears to be trying to confirm that surveillance is taking place.

On the Move: Subject of the surveillance is moving, on either foot or mobile.

Point: This term is used to identify the individual or team that will be leading the surveillance at various times during the operation.

Raised Up: The subject of the surveillance appears to be aware that they are the subject of surveillance.

Squaring the Block: Squaring is a tactic whereby the subject will make three or more turns in the same area, usually three lefts or three rights, to square the block and detect a tail.

Surveillance: Surveillance can be defined as the monitoring of behavior or as the secretive and continuous observance of an individual's activities. The word *surveillance* in French means "watching over." What I am talking about with respect to doing surveillance is the secret observation of persons, places, or things as an investigative technique.

Surveillance Intelligence: This is useful information obtained during surveillance that could aid in successful future surveillances or a successful investigation.

Tail: The investigator assigned to take the lead or the point in following the person of interest can be known as the "tail." Any member of the team can assume this position during the course of surveillance.

Target: Person, place, or thing being surveilled. Other terms used in place of "target" might be "Subject" or "Person of Interest" (POI).

CHAPTER 2
Someone to Watch Over
As I grow older, I pay less attention to what men say.
I just watch what they do.
Andrew Carnegie[1]

The use of surveillance has been an invaluable tool in the fight against corruption. The skill may be used to obtain probable cause for search warrants, develop other investigative leads, identify co-conspirators, gather intelligence, and locate persons and things.

The purpose of surveillance is to obtain information difficult to secure in any other manner. In most instances, the information needed is evidence of a crime, rule violation, or intelligence that may lead to the evidence of the crime being investigated.

Surveillance is an invaluable tool in helping to locate persons by watching their hangouts and associates or locating hidden property. It is also through surveillance that the reliability of informants can be confirmed. Surveillance is a powerful tool in helping to obtain information for later use in interrogations or interviews.

Basics

The information provided in this undertaking merely touches on the basics of surveillance. To fully present the awesome tool that surveillance is would require several volumes.

---

[1] Anderson, *Great Quotes from Great Leaders*, 39.

Please keep in mind that as technology improves and conspirators are better equipped to link their corrupt schemes, the way in which an investigator will approach surveillance of these individuals must change in order to keep pace with the changing environment. In the twenty-first century, surveillance must be approached with an ever-changing mind-set.

The art of surveillance requires competent and proven surveillance practices and procedures. Be mindful of the fact that the techniques used will be largely driven by the geography in which the operation takes place.

In my four decades of experience, I have found that no facet of investigative work is more susceptible to improvement through practice than those techniques used in conducting surveillance.

A Boring Undertaking

Surveillance can be boring. This boredom has a tendency to negatively affect an investigator's attention when conducting surveillance where little activity is taking place. Let me state, loud and clear: Boredom is the enemy. Like most enemies, it has a tendency to attack when least expected. Boredom can result in physical harm to the team.

I have had instances where investigators have fallen asleep during surveillance. I have also had investigators chased by targets with bats, crowbars, and trash cans because the team was not paying attention to their surroundings.

Just because there is information that a target might be at a location for several hours, is not an invitation to become inattentive. Surveillance is not a time for girl- or guy-watching, sunbathing, or watching movies on a smartphone, laptop, or tablet.

I recall a situation where an investigator had fallen into such a deep sleep that when he awoke, he had to call another team member to ask where he was. Such behavior is unacceptable, but that does not mean it will not happen.

Properly executed surveillance is often the investigative step that will take down long-running conspiracies. In fact, I recall managing a fourteen-million-dollar heating oil fraud investigation that owes its success in large part to the surveillance task force put together to monitor the activities of heating-oil trucks from the point of loading the product to the trucks' return to the depot. The scheme began to unravel after comparing surveillance reports with invoices for purchases of heating oil.

Please take note that there is a significant difference in following tractor-trailer-type trucks as opposed to cars. In a tractor, the driver is usually sitting up high, with a much more expansive view of the area. This expanded view increases the possibility that the driver will detect the vehicles that follow.

It is always best to conduct a multicar operation when following these types of vehicles and to switch the point as often as possible.

CHAPTER 3
The What-If Process
"You will not solve a problem with the same mindset that created it."
Vinny Green

In all of the training in which an investigator is involved, as well as just simple everyday life, it is imperative that a WIP mind-set is always engaged. WIP means "What If Process." WIP is the thought process that has the potential to save your life in most any setting. It is an absolute must in a surveillance setting.

WIP is not rocket science; the practice is just a common-sense approach that team members must employ daily for their entire law enforcement career and beyond.

The gospel, according to WIP, simply says that it would be foolish to wait for a negative situation to unfold in front of us and then try to prepare a plan of action on the fly.

Because of the conditions in which we currently live, especially in surveillance settings, we must engage the WIP mind-set once the good Lord allows our feet to touch the floor each day.

It is at this point that we must begin thinking about how to respond to situations, such as being burned. If we wait until it happens, it is far too late to think about an effective and successful response. As a result, an investigator will be reduced to a scatter-mob reaction in an attempt to protect themselves and protect the team.

When everything goes to hell in a handbasket, an investigator will find that there is little time, if any, to implement a split-second reaction plan to protect the team.

This lack of time is why a response plan must already be in place in your mind and, when possible, shared with the team and discussed in detail. In this profession, it is always better to respond than to react.

Reactions are usually instinctive and may be well suited for battle that an investigator did not plan on or anticipate. However, responses are more often reasoned and planned and, therefore, likely to be more appropriate for unexpected confrontations of the type that an investigator may encounter during surveillance.

Most encounters that an investigator will face during a surveillance confrontation will take place on the target's playing field, either their neighborhood, place of business, or somewhere frequented where there will be many friends. The team must prepare for this eventuality and plan for it ahead of time.

Before an investigator hits the street, the primary question to ask would be what if this or that happens. Just thinking about it begins the response process.

Let that process begin with the fact that most investigators will have access to the potential safety of their vehicle. Do not abandon safe ground. A physical fight should be the final step in the confrontation process and should only take place when all other options have failed. It makes no sense to get out of the safety of a vehicle or confront a person whose skill set is unknown.

I recall the first day of defensive tactics training when I was an investigator. The instructor asked the class this question: "Who took fourth place in Judo during the summer Olympics?"

No one could answer the question. Someone in the dojo might have known who took the first or second place. However, it is rare that anyone remembers the fourth-place person in an event.

We all wondered why he was asking the question. The answer was not complicated: If an investigator does not know who took fourth place in judo during the Olympics then, it is not a stretch for that Olympian to be the person the investigator is about to battle. In the alternative, the individual could at least be someone with an equal skill set. Despite the saying, ignorance is not always bliss.

The point is that an investigator seldom knows the skill level of the person challenging their authority. In this profession, there is no advanced notice of a need to use force. The closest thing there is to having advance knowledge of an opponent is training, and a well thought out WIP. It is all about responding over reacting.

CHAPTER 4
You Are Not the Only One Watching
"Nothing in life happens in a vacuum."
Vinny Green

When conducting surveillance, always be mindful of the fact that an investigator's presence in an area can draw attention. Take the time to employ counter surveillance techniques to see who is watching the team's activities. This is especially concerning in residential areas or areas frequented by the same people. "If you don't belong, make yourself small."

I can recall an incident where a surveillance team was set up at a large bus depot. During the course of that surveillance, someone from an upper floor at the location fired a weapon at the surveillance vehicle, striking the windshield twice.

In another instance, a colleague of mine was on surveillance and was detected by the target. The target of the surveillance struck the investigator with his vehicle. The investigator's injuries included a broken leg.

In yet another instance, the surveillance team was observing a target that was about to drive a public bus after having consumed large amounts of alcohol in a bar. When the team came out of the establishment, they found the surveillance vehicle on fire.

Dealing with misconduct by government employees can result in a host of reactions from these individuals. Those reactions, without a doubt, can place an investigator in harm's way.

Surveillance Options

When conducting surveillance, an investigator has essentially three options available in order to complete the task. Those options are electronic surveillance, stationary surveillance, or moving surveillance (through use of a vehicle or following the target on foot).

Electronic Surveillance

With the increase in technological advancements, the use of electronic surveillance techniques has increased. There are three types of electronic surveillance commonly used during fraud investigations. These are wiretapping, bugging, and videotaping.

Wiretapping is mainly used when there are strong indications that conversations concerning corruption conspiracies are taking place over the telephone or cell phone. If evidence is compelling, it is possible to obtain a court-ordered warrant for a wiretap.

Another electronic surveillance technique used is what is commonly called "bugging." Bugging takes place by secretly placing listening devices at a location with the intent of secretly listening to and recording conversations to obtain evidence of a corruption conspiracy. This can also be done using video surveillance in which cameras are hidden in the same way as microphones in order to record transactions and conversations that may produce evidence of a crime.

It is essential to conduct the appropriate analysis to determine what can be done legally with respect to electronic surveillance. Take the time to determine if there is an expectation of privacy and if a court order is needed to conduct this type of surveillance.

Do not take this lightly or, for that matter, make decisions based solely on a previous matter. In any operation, privacy can be a tricky thing. In many jurisdictions, placing an electronic device in place to monitor a cubicle is not the same as monitoring an office.

Monitoring an office that has a door, as opposed to one that does not have a door, can change the entire way in which electronic surveillance can be legally conducted. The presence of the door suggests that the office occupant may have an expectation of privacy. Similar expectations may apply to file cabinets and desk drawers, even when the organization owns those items and an employee may be using them.

Stationary Surveillance

Stationary surveillance is not unusual in conducting corruption investigations. It is used when there is no expectation that the subject will be moving during the day. This can happen when the investigation is working to document meetings that are taking place.

It could also occur when an individual is not doing their job, and instead goes somewhere unrelated to their employment and hangs out for the day.

Early in my career, I spent weeks at a time at the horseracing track or off-track betting parlors watching employees spend the entire workday placing bets and then filing false reports about their daily activity.

Fourth Amendment Protects People, Not Places

The Fourth Amendment to the US Constitution only protects against searches that violate a reasonable expectation of privacy. In the United States, a reasonable expectation of privacy exists:
1) If an individual actually expects privacy and

2) If an individual's expectation is one that society as a whole would think is legitimate.

    This opinion comes from a decision by the United States Supreme Court in 1967, Katz v. United States, holding that when a person enters a telephone booth, shuts the door, and makes a call, the government cannot record what that person says on the phone without a warrant. (This case took place during a time when public telephones were in abundance and encased within a box that the user could step into, close an accordion-type door, and place a call for a nominal fee.)

    Even though the recording device was stuck to the outside of the phone booth glass and did not physically invade Katz's private space, the Supreme Court decided that when Katz shut the booth's door, he justifiably expected that no one would hear his conversation. It was this expectation— rather than the inside of the phone booth itself—that was protected from government intrusion by the Fourth Amendment. This idea is generally phrased as "the Fourth Amendment protects people, not places."[2]

---

[2] Surveillance Self-Defense, "Reasonable Expectation of Privacy."

CHAPTER 5
Moving Surveillance
"Far too many of us plan for the positive but are intent on walking in the negative."
Vinny Green

Moving surveillance is a method of surveillance used when the target of the surveillance is moving and is likely to move for the better part of the surveillance operation, either on foot or in a vehicle.

Make sure that there are enough members on the surveillance team to continue the surveillance in the event that the subject makes use of public transportation or some other mode of transportation other than a personal or business vehicle.

When conducting a fixed or mobile surveillance, the following tactics are available to the team:

➢ *Close:* When following an individual in a congested area, it is best to keep in close contact with the target. In cases such as these, it is recommended to use fixed objects and uninvolved people as blocks between the team and the target. It is of utmost importance that this is done in a discreet manner so as not to draw attention to the surveillance team or the focus of the surveillance.
➢ *Loose:* A loose surveillance is used when extreme caution is necessary. It is also used when the target is in an area where a close surveillance would leave investigators open to being detected.

In a loose surveillance, the investigator should attempt to take note of all possible escape routes in the area that the target might use. This is done in the event that the distance from the target does not allow for a constant visual.

> ➤ **Chain:** Chain surveillance is done when extreme caution is necessary and there is a sense of where the target is going. An example is as follows:

- The first investigator following the target will take the point from home and drop the target when it is reasonably certain that the target's destination is the known work location or a location that is known to the team.
- A second investigator will pick the target up at this location, and another investigator will reestablish visual contact from this location.

This method is commonly used when a number of surveillances have been conducted and a set pattern has been determined. This is a type of surveillance that requires detailed teamwork and communication.

Techniques to Use in Conducting Surveillance

Leapfrog

Employment of this method can be done in "foot" surveillance or "auto" surveillance. It requires the participation of a minimum of three individuals with either method that is chosen. The target is kept in view by the first investigator, with the remainder of the team following behind. After an agreed-upon period, the second investigator replaces the first, who, in turn, takes up a position in the rear.

An automobile is kept available to pick up an investigator and transport them in the event the target enters a vehicle, thereby terminating surveillance on foot.

If the target being followed is in a vehicle, the same basic strategy is used for leapfrogging, except that the vehicles now change positions with one another in the same way that the investigators on foot were doing.

Leapfrogging vehicles requires practice and an understanding of traffic conditions and the general area in which the surveillance might take place. Employing defensive driving techniques is a must.

A.B.C. or Group Method on Foot

This is similar to the leapfrog method, except an attempt is made to keep the target in sight at all times by all members of the surveillance team. Besides tailing the target, who would be designated as "A" in this method, one investigator, "B," would follow from the rear. The "C" investigator would observe the target from across the street, thus bracketing the target and providing the investigators with a particularly strategic position from which to observe the target, especially when the target turns corners and reverses their direction.

Parallel Method

This is similar to the A.B.C. group method except that in this case, vehicles are positioned behind the target and on parallel streets moving in the same direction.

Preparation

Prior to beginning the surveillance, all participants should be thoroughly briefed. The background of the individual being surveilled should be evaluated. The object of the surveillance should be well established, and any possible contingencies that might arise should be thoroughly examined.

Prior to any operation, research must be done. This includes conducting a full workup on the subject. This workup must include a criminal history check.

This information is critical. It can give the team a sense of how the target may respond if he detects the surveillance. It also provides the team with an idea of the types of individuals that the target may associate with and neighborhoods that they may frequent.

This information will help in preparing for the surveillance and addressing the need for any backup plans or notification to other law enforcement entities that might be in the area or able to provide assistance if things do not go as planned.

In an effort to determine locations the target might frequent or visit from time to time, it is a wise idea to review parking summonses that have been issued to vehicles registered to the target or vehicles that might be driven on a regular basis. Keep in mind that if the target is not the only one driving the vehicle, those summonses may have nothing to do with the target.

If Lexis/Nexis, Westlaw, or similar databases are available, they are worthwhile sources of information. However, as with any information obtained, always double-check the facts.

These databases could also provide information concerning businesses that the target may own, and places of residency that might not be found in a personnel folder. They could also alert the team to names and addresses of relatives of the target.

Photos and Social Media

Having a current photograph of the surveillance target is a vital part of the surveillance package. Photographs can come from personnel files or employee ID systems. Be aware of the possibility of these photographs being several years old.

In the twenty-first century, a useful source of photographs is from the various social networks available on the Internet. However, do not rely on social networks as the only source of information for such items as photographs. Government sources that maintain any type of license or permit are also a potential source of intelligence.

A comment about social networks: Most people are not as security-conscious as they think they are in this area. If current information is needed on an individual, try opening a covert account on a social network and seek to become friends or connected with the target.

In a significant percentage of cases, the target will be more than willing to add a member of the team to their list of hundreds of social network friends. Ego plays a big part in this. Many people like to brag about how many friends or contacts they have. Use this ego trip to the team's advantage.

This approach also gives the team access to the target's friends and most likely a whole host of photographs and information that would be helpful in conducting the investigation.

CHAPTER 6
Communication and Information
"Never try to beat your opponent; instead, always try to beat yourself."
Vinny Green

Take the time and make sure to establish a communications base station, where the team can call into for information. This should be separate from the organization's routine communications used on a daily basis. It is important that surveillance teams not be hindered in making contact with base during a surveillance.

Allowing the surveillance base station to be used for assignments other than the day's surveillance could be detrimental to the team and the assignment overall.

Something that is not routinely done by all corruption-fighting agencies is advance surveillance on the target's home or locations that the surveillance may include. This is actually a valuable step in the preparation process and will provide the team with information that cannot be obtained anywhere else.

Sometimes preparation requires getting up from a desk and taking the initiative to see things firsthand. This includes supervisors, as well as the team in the field.

For a supervisor, it is much easier to make a decision about what to do on surveillance if the supervisor can visualize the location before making a decision. A pre-surveillance will provide that benefit.

Information obtained during the pre-surveillance should include details on the area where the operation will be taking place:

- Is the area residential, commercial, or a combination?
- Are restricted parking regulations in effect in the area?
- If parking regulations are in effect, what are the times and days that they are in effect?
- Is the target located on a one- or two-way street?

Information such as these is critical when making a decision on where to place surveillance vehicles or team members on foot.

The pre-surveillance will provide information on how many exits there are that the target might have an opportunity to use at various locations. The pre-surveillance should be conducted within two or three days of the actual surveillance. This makes it close to real time, affording the team the opportunity to determine such factors as construction taking place, which might affect surveillance operations.

Investigators involved should be familiar with the probable locations that the surveillance might take the team to during the operation. Areas such as the target's work location, residence, children's schools, and the transportation facilities serving these locations are areas that the surveillance team should have detailed information on for possible use during the operation.

Knowledge of the buildings in the area, types of occupancy, and character of the population are of utmost importance. Make sure that the team fits into the neighborhood.

Investigators should avail themselves beforehand of any equipment they are likely to need, such as electronic devices, signaling equipment, disguises, vehicles, credentials, cameras, badges, uniforms, and photographs.

A few words of advice: When assigned to conduct surveillance, avoid participating in functions that may lead to drinking alcohol the night before or within a few hours of the operation. Simply put, alcohol impairs judgment. The thing about impaired judgment is that you do not know your judgment is impaired until you make the wrong decision.

Most surveillances involve driving of a motor vehicle at some point during the operation; alcohol will affect driving skills and reflexes. No matter how good you think your driving skills may be, a competent and skilled investigator would never want to imbibe in the use of alcoholic beverages and then test this belief. There is no substitute for safety.

Identification of Target

Positive identification of the target is essential for obvious reasons. An effort should be made to observe the target before the operation begins; it is a real-time observation and is better than a photograph or video.

When providing descriptions of the target to team members, include peculiarities such as gait, habits, and places frequented. Provide the type of details that will be helpful during the surveillance. Every trait is significant, particularly the ones that make the target stand out.

While eye and hair color may be routine, a nose or lip ring would be helpful in confirming the identity of the subject. When describing what the target is wearing, take the time to point out the holes in their jeans or the fact that they usually wear four rings on their left hand.

Become thoroughly familiar with the individual's appearance from the rear, as this is the position from which they will generally be observed. Are there any bulges in their pockets, holes in their sneakers, unusual haircuts, belts, or keys hanging from their pants?

It is also important to try to obtain information on the occupants in the target's household. There are times when relatives occupying the household may be similar in appearance to the target. I can share several instances where investigators followed brothers or cousins of targets because of a lack of research by the team in knowing who was in the household.

Investigators need to know all of the possibilities that may present themselves during the course of the surveillance. Do the necessary research!

CHAPTER 7
The Making of a Successful Surveillance
"Where doth exist the antidote to indifference, more to the point, who among us is willing to swallow?"
Vinny Green

Conducting surveillance is more than just people getting together with a few pairs of binoculars. It requires serious preparation and an understanding of the obstacles that an investigator will have to confront during the surveillance operation. Success does not require being a superhero, but it does require being super-prepared.

Restrooms: Speaking frankly, an investigator may be spending many hours crossing his or her legs in an effort to keep bodily functions at bay. The luxury of a bathroom may not be available while on a surveillance operation.

A veteran detective once shared this bit of wisdom with me: If an investigator is doing early-morning surveillance, get up two to three hours before planning to leave the house. This way, an individual's normal bodily functions have been addressed before the surveillance begins.

We all need to be serious when it comes down to comfort and life's routine needs. The need for access to bathroom facilities is not always going to be a possibility. Finding a restroom is sometimes difficult to do, and it is hard to find the time to do while out on surveillance. It will often require an investigator to be resourceful and think outside of the box.

If bathroom facilities are needed and available, notify all of the team members that a personal break is being taken. Make sure to take communication devices in order to stay in contact with the team in the event that the target goes mobile. Be prepared to be left behind.

An investigator must be mindful of any conversations they may have in the bathroom using communication devices. It is not likely that the luxury of seeing everyone in the bathroom or, for that matter, knowing who these people are will exist.

Food: Lunch breaks are rare during surveillance operations, and there is not always an opportunity to stop and buy anything. Packing food and drink as a part of a surveillance kit is a smart idea. However, keep in mind that drinking too much will result in a need to use the bathroom, and we have already discussed the potential problems with that need.

Tail: The investigator following the target must make every effort to be inconspicuous. Be aware of the environment and surroundings. Remember, people are always watching.

Even people who have nothing to do with the operation have the potential of compromising a team member because of concerns about unfamiliar people in the neighborhood; Grandma is always looking out of the window.

If law enforcement or a civilian approaches, have a story prepared beforehand. Be particularly wary of children and animals; they are curious and are not bashful about approaching someone who has been hanging around for a long time.

Dress for Success: Dressing for success applies to individual investigators, the entire team, and even the vehicles in use. Team members should be conservative in the way that they dress. Make sure that the clothing fits any environment that the surveillance may take the team.

Equipment: Pay attention to equipment issues. Failure to do so will cost time when it simply cannot be wasted. Laziness will cause the team pain.

Always have a full tank of gas prior to the operation and the means to acquire more gas quickly. Do not wait for the tank to be close to empty; start thinking about filling up when the tank is on the halfway point.

Have a Global Positioning System (GPS) device in the car. This piece of equipment is an investment. Do not invest in junk. Believe it or not, maps still exist and are an excellent resource during surveillance. However, in the twenty-first century, whenever possible, financially and tactically, GPS is the way to go, and a map should be available as a backup in the event of the GPS not working.

The Little Things

Surveillance will not stop because a GPS has lost a signal or is broken. It also will not stop because of inclement weather. However, the surveillance will stop if vehicle wiper blades are in poor condition and fail to keep the windshield clear during surveillance in inclement weather. Take the time to do a physical inspection of the vehicle, including such items as wiper blades, proper inflation of tires, and bubbles and wear on the tires. Take the time to feel the tires for foreign objects.

Bypassing the little things can cause a miserable day. Take the time and check vehicle headlights, taillights, and brake lights. If any of these lights are not working, there is potential for being noticed, especially in nighttime surveillance. Being pulled over by other law enforcement Officials unaware that an operation is taking place is also a possibility.

Try to avoid using vehicles that do not fit into the neighborhood or have noticeable dents, bumper stickers, or other distinguishing marks that will make the vehicle memorable. If any of the aforementioned observations are made concerning the target's vehicle, use this information to help maintain a visual on the vehicle.

31

CHAPTER 8
Upon Arrival at the Surveillance Starting Point
"If my peace depends on external realities, then it is not actually my peace."
Vinny Green

Once the surveillance begins, be mindful of the possibility of the subject's residence having more than one exit; these include exits from a garage.

If it is determined that the team is unable to set up within the immediate vicinity, the team should work to determine the choke points in the area. Determine how many ways the target can leave their home or the surveillance starting point. Then set up teams at those points. Remember, surveillance is a team sport. Everyone has a position and an assignment.

Not every member of the team is supposed to see everything that is going on. Communication keeps everyone informed. Trying to operate any other way is likely to jeopardize the operation.

When a team member has the "eye," meaning the team member who has taken the lead in following the target, they must communicate and paint a visual picture for the other team members. It is everyone's responsibility to communicate with the team.

In an effort to be the best that I can be and, in turn, allow my staff to be the best that they can be, I have taken the initiative to become a certified defensive driving instructor. I provide defensive driving instruction to my G-Square staff as needed. We all have a responsibility to be a defensive driver. We are not the only drivers on the road, and surveillance does not take priority over safety.

We must utilize rear- and side-view mirrors to observe the target's movements. Keep in mind that several things will be going on during surveillance, such as photography and radio communication. All of these things can be distracting. Be safe and drive carefully; there will always be another day.

It is strongly suggested that there be a policy of not running red lights and demonstrating extreme caution at yellow lights. Also, do not get in the habit of accelerating as soon as the light turns green. You never know if the oncoming driver has a practice of accelerating when they see the light turning red on their side.

Tailing Teams

A one-man tail is difficult and increases the possibility of detection. The number of tails per team depends on the type of surveillance being conducted and the complexity of the investigation.

The usual number for a surveillance team is two or three investigators to ensure an effective surveillance. Be sensitive to the distance between the target and the investigator assigned to tail the target.

There is no specific rule. Distance depends upon the number of persons on the street; time of day or night; type of area; whether it is a close, loose, or chain surveillance; and the surveillance skills of the operative.

A beneficial general rule to follow is to shorten distances in crowds or when the target approaches a bus, train, or taxi; lengthen distances in sparsely occupied areas.

If the Target Is Lost

Generally, there is more than one tail assigned to a target. When a target has been lost, immediately contact other team members and notify the base station, giving the last-known location of the target.

It is possible to second-guess the target. Having knowledge of habits and paying attention to established patterns, may enable the team to proceed to where the subject's next location may be, thereby re-establish contact.

For instance, clues may come from regular visits to a location, business, places of entertainment, interacting with associates, and so on, all in conjunction with the day of the week and the time of the day.

How to Respond When Burned

There may come a time when the target of the surveillance will detect the surveillance. When this happens, act as natural as possible. One method used to detect surveillance is for the target to window-shop. Using plate glass windows as mirrors to detect surveillance is a common tactic used by targets who are sensitive to surveillances being conducted.

If there is suspicion of having been burned, take measures to have another member of the team pick up the tail, or if appropriate, terminate the surveillance for the day. When the replacement makes contact, "drop" the tail.

Another method an individual might use is one of confrontation in order to observe reactions. If this happens, never surrender and never appear guilty. Always plan for this possibility and have a low-key response prepared. Never invoke a response that will draw attention or make you more memorable than you already have been.

If the target attempts to double back, do not be caught off guard. Show no signs of confusion, employ WIP, and act as natural as possible.

Do not return to other team members. The target may be watching or even have someone else watching on their behalf. Keep in mind that in many circumstances, it might be best to discontinue the surveillance if there is a strong indication that the target has detected the operation.

The best procedure to follow is to contact the base station or other team members, giving the target's location so that one of the team members can get on the target's tail. In doing this, notify the base station and team of the route and approximate point and time at which the relief picked up the tail on the target.

Auto Tailing

Each team should have communication devices available, such as cellphones and radio communication. If one of the techniques already discussed is not in use, a method to use would be to have the first car tailing keep the other cars informed of travel direction, turns, and stops of the target. The other car(s) should proceed on a parallel route and be available to take the lead when directed to do so.

At a minimum, there should be two-person teams in each vehicle; one drives, and the other observes and takes notes. When following the target to an area where parking the vehicle is required, it is usually best to alight from the vehicle to give the impression there is a reason for being there.

Use two or more autos, alternating positions. If this is going to be a multiday surveillance, attempt to change autos daily. Get in the habit of having binoculars, cameras, and maps in all vehicles.

There are times when an agency's budget will not allow for multiple vehicles in order to change vehicles for surveillances. In these instances, consider renting cars. This option will allow vehicles to be changed on a regular basis.

Another tool an investigator may want to add to the surveillance arsenal is to have a switch in the surveillance vehicle to be used for nighttime highway surveillances. This switch will turn one of the vehicle's headlights off and on, so if the individual being followed becomes suspicious when they look in their rearview mirror, they will not always see two headlights following and may not realize that it is the same vehicle. Needless to say, do not activate the switch where the target will see the light turning on or off.

Available Resources

I have found that establishing a relationship with the property clerk's office with the local police department might provide investigators with the opportunity to borrow equipment, such as vehicles, bicycles, and other equipment, that will help on surveillance.

A note about borrowing property from the property clerk's office: Do a full inspection of the property borrowed. I recall an operation where we borrowed bicycles from the property clerk's office. When we were unloading the bikes from the transport van, one of the bikes fell, and the handlebars struck the ground, and several packets of cocaine fell out.

In another instance, we borrowed a vehicle from the property clerk's office, during the operation, one of the vehicle's tires went flat. When we took the tire in for repair, the repairperson opened the tire and found it full of drugs.

Do not forget the fact that these items are in the clerk's possession in relation to an alleged crime having been committed. Check the borrowed items from top to bottom.

If the resources are unavailable, consider trading with another agency. If neither of these options is possible, then change the look of the vehicles being used. When possible, alternate positions in the vehicle.

Keep within the same street as the target's car; this helps to reduce the chance of being caught at traffic lights. Be cautious of the fact that cigarettes or cigars lit in parked autos and engines running arouse suspicion at night.

If the budget allows for it, invest in a surveillance van. Such a van is an investment that will yield benefits on any surveillances and those where investigators just cannot be seen.

Members of my technical squad built the first surveillance van that I used. We obtained an impounded cargo van from the police impound yard, wood from a construction site, and various pieces of technical equipment from stores such as RadioShack and the like. It was a very inexpensive tool to build. A well-equipped surveillance van can be parked at a location, with a team in the back unseen to observe all of the activity in the area.

CHAPTER 9
Public Transportation
"People don't lose hope; they choose to leave it behind."
Vinny Green

When conducting surveillance in urban areas, it is prudent to plan for the possibility of the surveillance ending up on public transportation at some point. This could be a bus, bike, express bus, Citi Bike, scooters, train, Uber, taxi, tour bus, or any of the various types of transportation available in an urban setting.

Because this possibility exists, it is an appropriate tactic for all team members to have public transportation access paraphernalia or funds available for any mode of transportation that the target may use.

Buses and Trains

In addition to having one or more tails on the bus, have surveillance vehicles in place to follow the bus. Investigators should be mindful that in the 21st century, "Bus Lanes" are found in many urban areas which can contribute to difficulty in conducting surveillance.

Be mindful of the fact that in many urban centers, there are specific traffic rules that favor buses. These rules could result in surveillance teams on foot or in other vehicles having difficulty keeping contact with targets on buses. The congestion that exists in subway systems will also make it difficult to maintain a visual on a target.

An effective technique is to enter the bus or train as closely behind the target as possible. Have another team member enter as well as a safety valve in the event the point feels burned. In employing this technique, make an effort to pass the target unnoticed as they are taking a seat.

Generally, stand or sit to the rear of the target if possible. Leave the bus or train with the target, but not immediately behind them. If it is possible, try to remain seated when the target is standing near the door; this way there will be no surprise if the target suddenly returns to their seat in an attempt to detect the surveillance.

Taxicabs

Some of the techniques and pitfalls used in following taxicabs are similar to those found in conducting surveillance on other public transportation. Just as with buses and trains, there are traffic conditions that favor taxicabs, such as dispatch stations at airports and bus and train terminals that limit access to taxicabs only.

In addition, at dispatch stations located at airports and train stations, there can be a large number of taxicabs conducting business. Losing sight of a taxi that a target may be occupying is not uncommon.

As soon as the target gets into a taxi, be sure to get the medallion number of the taxi. The number is usually on the top of the cab and visible from the outside. The medallion number will be helpful when trying to keep track of the vehicle in congested areas. It will also be helpful in the event that there is a need to obtain the taxi's trip card at a later date to determine the subject's destination.

In the event that a team member has to take a taxi in order to keep the target in view, direct the taxi driver to stay within the same street as the tailed taxi. While this is seen in many movies and television shows, having one taxi follow another is not the best approach to use. However, there are times that an investigator needs to improvise.

The rule of the day is to use wisdom in these instances. Consider if the taxi driver is likely to compromise the operation. The answer is usually no. It is rare that the taxi driver in the vehicle that is being followed will take note of a tail. This means that it is unlikely that they will compromise the operation.

Similarly, it is not likely that the taxi driver following the target will take the time out of their day to compromise an operation. However, it is also not impossible, so be mindful and act accordingly. Keep conversations to a minimum with respect to communicating with other team members while in the taxi. Do not give away any information that will reveal the purpose of the surveillance or the identity of the target.

Citi Bike

Citi Bike is a privately owned public bicycle sharing system serving the New York City boroughs of Manhattan, Queens, and Brooklyn, as well as Jersey City, New Jersey. It is likely that programs such as these will expand to other cities.

The Citi Bike program and its offspring have or will relate to surveillance in two immediate ways, one being that it is an excellent vehicle for an investigator or the entire team to use on surveillance in urban settings. The other being that it is equally convenient to be used by the subject of a surveillance at a moment's notice.

Surveillance teams must be ready for this eventuality and have it factored into the surveillance plan, as well as having a debt or credit card available to use in renting a bike when needed.

Surveillance teams must also recognize that the limitations that come with driving a car are not the same as maneuvering on city streets with a bicycle.

Building Elevators

Elevators, escalators, and stairwells are all locations that can place an investigator in a position to be confronted by a target with nowhere for an investigator to go. Think about this when entering such locations.

Upon entering an elevator, always try to stand toward the rear of the target. Do not immediately press the button for a floor. Allow the subject to select their floor and then follow up from there.

If the situation allows for it, try to exit the elevator on the same floor as the target. If this is not possible, try to exit a floor above, and immediately take the stairs down to their floor and try to determine what location they entered.

Should the target observe the tail getting off the elevator, enter an office or knock on an apartment door on that floor and ask for a "Mr. Perry." In situations where an investigator is in an apartment building, pretend to be a salesperson or someone who would not be seen as totally out of place at the location. Have a name and a story at the ready.

If the target enters an office or apartment and does not observe the tail, note the location. This information should be included in the report documenting the day's activities.

If it becomes necessary to enter the same office with the target (close tail), do so, and endeavor to overhear their conversation. Normally, the tail will be waited upon shortly thereafter; when this happens, ask for the fictitious "Mr. Perry" or give a story of seeking employment.

Restaurants

Patronizing a restaurant is common during the course of surveillance. Do not become a glutton because the boss is paying. Remember, there is an operation in play; do not get lost in the salad.

One of the first things that must be done is to ensure that all exits are covered from the outside. If it becomes necessary to enter the restaurant, sit toward the rear of the target. Order after they have done so and order an ordinary meal that the cook can prepare quickly. Begin eating after the target starts; try to finish before the target and obtain the check for the meal before the target does. If feasible, leave slightly before the target to allow the team to be ready to move when the target exits the restaurant.

CHAPTER 10
Reports
"We are not byproducts of our environment.
We are the products of our choices to our environment."
Vinny Green

In the twenty-first century, technology like smartphones and tablets are useful in maintaining notes to be used for preparing surveillance reports. If these are not available, stiff-backed file cards (3" × 5") are a tried-and-true method of recording surveillance notes. Try to keep them in chronological order.

Remember, this is a team effort. This means that nothing should take place independent of the team. Surveillance is probably more of a team effort than anything else in the investigative realm. It is the responsibility of the team member designated to write the report to read all of the surveillance notes taken by the team during the surveillance.

It is from these notes that the report will be constructed. Be certain that all notes are understood before beginning the writing process. Understanding the notes means that in preparing the report, an investigator must recognize that this requires input from all participants in the surveillance. It is imperative to communicate all of the facts and have these facts written in a clear and concise manner, easily understandable by the intended audience.

The report should not only include information on the day's events, but also take the time to document any video taken, photographs, or any documents obtained during the course of the **surveillance**.

The report needs to be set up similar to other reports that have been written, meaning that there needs to be consistency and a respect for the basics—who, where, what, when, why, and how sections.

Entries in the report should be recorded in a time-line format; beginning with what time the surveillance began. Each event should be accompanied by the corresponding time and location.

The report should include the names and titles of all surveillance team participants, including those in the field, as well as those covering the base station or research positions.

The written report should begin with a surveillance summary, describing the purpose and the results of the operation. The report needs to be a narrative of what was observed, and information obtained by all parties. The report should be as detailed as possible, including the target's reactions to various events during the day.

If the target engaged in misconduct, be sure to document the misconduct, and refer to any rulebooks that support the position that it is an infraction of the rules.

These reports should be reviewed by each tailing team for familiarization with the target's habits, patterns, new contacts, and other information that may be useful during any future surveillance. Taking this step will be helpful in avoiding duplication of effort in identifying new contacts or changes in the target's behavior.

There should be one surveillance report written by each team, and each team member is to sign off on that report. Do not have several reports written by each team member; this could lead to unnecessary confusion.

It is essential that all handwritten notes be attached to the typed surveillance report. Referencing these notes may become necessary at trial or any hearing that may take place. Having access to the notes during testimony will make it easier to recall who saw what. There should be a debriefing meeting with all team members at the conclusion of the day's surveillance operation. This means the team that was in the field, as well as the next team that will be going out.

Surveillance can make or break a case. It is a tool that must be skillfully used. Failure to apply it properly comes at a cost.

G-SQUARE INTERNATIONAL TRAINING ACADEMY
888c 8th Avenue, New York, NY 10019
Suite 424
G-Square.org
GSCTraining@optimum.net
(917) 681-2810